Religion
VERSUS
RELATIONSHIP

DR. VIOLET WALLACE

PALMETTO
P U B L I S H I N G
Charleston, SC
www.PalmettoPublishing.com

Copyright © 2023 by Dr. Violet Wallace

All rights reserved

No portion of this book may be reproduced, stored in a retrieval system, or transmitted in any form by any means—electronic, mechanical, photocopy, recording, or other—except for brief quotations in printed reviews, without prior permission of the author.

Paperback ISBN: 979-8-8229-3188-6
eBook ISBN: 979-8-8229-3705-5

ACKNOWLEDGEMENTS

All praises belong to God for giving me the inspiration and insight to write *Religion Verses Relationship*. Pastor Lillian Johnson, I give you my appreciation for your editorial work in the preparation of the book. Thank you for your helpful development through the writing of this project. Many thanks to my children for giving me the opportunity to complete my assignment. Ashia Stewart, I am grateful for your support. My gratitude to Faith in Action Deliverance Ministries for their continued support and encouragement. Thanks to one and all.

INTRODUCTION

We have two homes. The earthly home in which we live in this world, and our heavenly home, which if we make it into, we live life eternally. **Matthew 7:13-14 (NKJV)** states, enter by the narrow gate; for wide is the gate and broad is the way that leads to destruction, and there are many who go in by it. Because narrow is the gate and difficult is the way which leads to life, there are few who find it. The world in which we live is temporal. Absolutely nothing in this world is permanent. King Solomon said it best in Ecclesiastes 1:14 (NKJV), when he stated, I have seen all the works that are done under the sun; and indeed, all *is* vanity and grasping for the wind. Just as we have a covenant marriage as husband and wife, we need a covenant relationship with Jesus Christ. Just as we are intimate in our marriages, we need to be intimate in our relationship with Jesus Christ. **Intimacy** is defined as a close familiarity or friendship; closeness. Intimacy refers to a level of closeness where you feel validated and safe. In relationships, there are four types of intimacy **emotional, physical, mental, and spiritual**. In its present tense we maintain a spiritual an intimate relationship with Jesus Christ. Not a form of religion. Mere religion is empty and worthless without a relationship! According to **Hebrews 11:8** Jesus Christ *is* the same yesterday, today, and forever. It is in a relationship with Christ we have eternal life. God has given us free will to choose a relationship with Him or the religions of this world. The decision is up to you. Choose whom you will serve in spirit and in truth. Make sure you know what is in the best interest of your **inner man**, which is your spirit man. As a born-again Christian, the conditions of your spirit will determine the quality of your life. God looks at the inner man according to **1Peter 3:4** (NKJV). If God be God, serve Him and for those who seek and serve, they must do so in spirit and in truth.

FOREWORD

This book *Religion Verses Relationship* is captivating. You do not want to put it down! It serves up an appetizer that you cannot get enough of, which leads to the main course so fulfilling with the knowledge of God. El Ohim is another name used for God.

Religion Verses Relationship explains in details what is the difference between the two systems. Religion has a form of godliness but is just a state of being alive. Having a personal, intimate relationship with God is spiritually living.

Religion Verses Relationship brings awareness of where you are positioned in Christ Jesus. What stance do you need to take to be in the right relationship? Is it going to be religion or relationship? The book empowers us with teachings on the different types of religion such as what ancient men and women worshipped and some practices still alive today. It's important to understand how other religions viewed Jesus Christ as another prophet but not Lord and savior of the world. How he was the one that was prophesied by the Old Testament prophets and being fulfilled in the New Testament, through his birth, death, and resurrection. There is tension between faith and religion (pg16). Faith is believing with spiritual confidence of God's existence rather than requiring proof. This is in contrast to religion that is believing there is a supreme power or being. Religion is in the mind and heart (pg24). It should not be about rules and regulations about who is right or wrong.

Religion is manmade and is based upon good work and self-gratifications. Relationships are based on living and obeying the word of God. Love is commitment. God expressed what a real relationship should be with Him. When we are connected to the vine, salvation takes place, deliverance and healing. The true identity of God is revealed. Jesus Christ, the bread of life, came down from heaven. He breaks down partitions and removed walls between us.

TABLE OF CONTENTS

Acknowledgements · iii
Introduction · 1
Foreword · 3

Chapter 1	Religion ·	7
	How it all Began ·	*17*
	Religious Babylon is the System · · · · · · · · · · · · · ·	*18*
	Universal Religion ·	*19*
Chapter 2	Relationship ·	20
Chapter 3	The Eschatology ·	26
Chapter 4	Where Is Your Relationship with Jesus Christ? · · · · · · · · ·	31
	Institutions of the World System · · · · · · · · · · · · · ·	*32*
	Which Church are You ·	*34*
Chapter 5	Before It's Too Late ·	37

Summary · 43
Vocabulary · 45
References · 50
About the Author · 53

Chapter 1
RELIGION

Some of the oldest religions in the world and the most practiced are Christianity, Buddhism, Hinduism, Islam, and Judaism. Christ is in the word Christianity and people have taken Christianity and extracted Christ from it to form their own religion instead of a true relationship with Jesus Christ.

The consent has already been given unto you. In Joshua 24:15, it states but if serving the Lord seems undesirable to you, then choose for yourselves this day whom you will serve, whether the gods your ancestors served beyond the Euphrates, or the gods of the Amorites, in whose land you are living. But as for me and my household, we will serve the Lord." Christianity, Islam, Hinduism, Buddhism, and Judaism are influential religions and comprise "big five" world religions. (Mary Gormandy White, M.A., Staff Writer).

The Christian religion is practiced most by believers. Christianity is implemented in many parts of the world. The United States, Mexico, Philippines, Africa, and Europe are some of the places where Christianity is practiced. Christianity is prudent to be the largest religion in the world. There are many categories of Christianity. Protestant and Catholicism denominations are categories encompassed in Christianity.

The United States is home to the largest population that practices Christianity. There are more than two billion believers' worldwide. The percentage of people that are Islam who practice Christianity is 23.2%, 15% Hinduism, 7.1% Buddhism, and 0.2% Judaism. (Mary Gormandy White, M.A., Staff Writer).

Those who believe in and practice Christianity believe in a monotheistic religion. Their belief is that there is only one true God. Praise and worship are important in their religion, and they believe in the Holy Trinity, the Father (God), the Son (Jesus), and the Holy Spirit, are all one. John 1:1 (NKJV) states in the beginning was the Word, and the Word was with God, and the Word was God. The Word of God, also known to humanity as the Bible, has sixty-six books and is the foundation of Christian teachings. Christians believe that Jesus Christ is the Son of God; he was crucified on a cross, died, was buried, and was resurrected to save humanity from their sins. After being entombed for three days, (Friday, Saturday, and Sunday) Jesus rose from the dead and ascended from Earth to heaven to be reunited with God. While in the process, Jesus took the keys of death, hell, and the grave and set those in bondage free. Romans 8:34 (NKJV) states, "Jesus is at the right hand of God and is also interceding for us." Christians have faith that there will be a second coming in which Jesus will return to Earth and take Christians back to heaven with him. The day and hour of Christ's return is not known to man or the angels, but the coming of the Lord is certain to take place when He returns in the rapture. "The Christianity of the Bible is a historical faith, exclusive and unique. I do not merely mean that it has its roots in human history; it is an ancient religion. Of course, it is but other religions can also claim the same thing. Hinduism, Islam, and Paganism are ancient religions. If we go back into the annals of history, we can find countless men and women worshipping the sun, moon, stars, animals, bugs, and men. [It] is an ancient religion" (Romans 1:18-32). (Schortmann, 2020, p. 6) It is with our mind that we serve God. What we imagine and believe, we give it power even if it's not true, and we open doors to practice religion instead of establishing a relationship with Christ.

Islam is the second largest world religion. People who practice the Islamic religion are called Muslims, and their faith is in a monotheistic God called Allah. "This religion is believed to have begun in the 7th century BC." Algeria, Bangladesh, Egypt, Iran, Iraq, Turkey, and Pakistan are several countries where more than 90% of the population is Muslim. Some places adhere to the Islamic *Sharia law*. A mosque is the name of the place of worship for Muslims. The Islamic religion teaches that Prophet Muhammad is Allah's final messenger, who continues to receive messages from Allah to share. The Islamic religion has a system called *caliphate*. Leaders operate within the system, and after the death of Muhammad, each leader is referenced to as *caliphs*. Sects are enveloped in the Islamic religion in that there are two major branches named *Sunnis* and *Shiites*. Muslims follow a strict prayer ritual by ensuring they pray five specific times throughout each day. They are also required to fast during the month of Ramadan and complete a pilgrimage to the holy city of Mecca at least once during their life span. Muslim women wear specific attire known as a *hijab* that covers their hair. They may also wear a *niqab* or *burka*, which cover up more of their appearance. The Quran is the Muslims' holy book.

Another world religion is Hinduism. Hinduism began on the subcontinent of India around 2300 BC. "As of 2018, 94% of those who follow the Hindu faith live in India" (White, Mary Gormandy, M.A., Staff Writer). The Hindu religion has their faith in different deities and consist of different sects. For example, Vaishnavism is devoted to the worship of the god Vishnu, and Shaivism is organized around worship of the god Shiva. "Brahman is the recognized supreme deity (god) responsible for creating everything in the universe. Brahman has no gender and is all-knowing and all-present." Hinduism instructs that god's presence exists in all of creation; god goes by many names and displays in infinite ways. Devas, known as demigods, are other Hindu deities. Also called devas, they have tremendous variations. It is important to note that none of their deities have died, been buried, or been resurrected. In addition, none of their deities have taken the keys from Hades or taken the sting out of death like Jesus Christ has done. Where are the deities, gods, and goddesses of religiosity? The Word of God shows us where Jesus is. Revelation 1:18 (NKJV) states I am He who lives, and was dead, and behold, I am alive forevermore. I have the keys of Hades and of death. While Christians believe in the indwelling of the holy spirit, Hinduism believe in a divine essence called *atman*, and it dwells within the individual that practices the Hindu religion. In Hinduism, sin has no end because they believe in reincarnation and there is a constant cycle of being born, living, and dying while on the path to enlightenment is a way of life to them.

According to Schortmann 2020, p. 7, 2 Corinthians 5:19-21 (NKJV) provides us with an understanding that God was in Christ reconciling the world to Himself, not counting their trespasses against them, and has committed to us the word of reconciliation. Therefore, we are ambassadors for Christ, as though God were making an appeal through us; we beg you on behalf of Christ to be reconciled to God. He made Him who knew no sin to be sin on our behalf, so that we might become the righteousness of God in Him.

Hinduism revolves around *karma*, which reflects on the good and bad deeds human do. If you do good, good will come back to you, or if you do something bad, then bad will come back to you. "Karma refers to the net of their good and bad deeds in the last life, and it determines the level into which they will be reborn" (White, Mary Gormandy, M.A., Staff Writer).

Hindus have various sacred texts they utilize as religious books. Some of their texts are entitled the *Vedas*, the *Samhitas*, the *Upanishads*, the *Ramayana*, and the *Bhagavad Gita*. Hindus believe cows are sacred and, as a result, eating beef is prohibited. Hindus also have *yoga* incorporated in their religious practices. Yoga requires one to empty their mind, while in Christianity, it is with our mind that we serve the Lord Jesus. After having been born again and becoming a new creature in Christ, our mind is renewed, and we no longer do things the old nature used to do.

Buddhism is another world religion and it was founded in the fifth century BC by Siddhartha Gautama. He lived a lavish lifestyle, and gave up his wealth, and live a life as a *monk*. He taught others to live in the same mannerism, and his enlightenment became the foundation of Buddhism. The Buddha should not be worshiped as a god. He was a man but not recognized by Buddhists as such."

Buddhists reside in the eastern and southeastern regions of Asia. Buddhists adhere to various traditions and methods. "*Theism* is not fundamental to Buddhism, though it is part of some traditions" (White, Mary Gormandy, M.A., Staff Writer). Buddhists believe in Karma, reincarnation, and rebirth. Buddhists have the perception that being "reincarnated means coming back as yourself multiple times, while rebirth involves returning as an entirely different entity." Buddhists abide by an avenue of moral living, thinking, behavior, and seeking wisdom. One who practices Buddhism must refrain from five precepts of killing, stealing, lying, misusing sex, and using drugs or alcohol. There are several sacred writings in the form of scriptures and texts that are affiliated with the Buddhists philosophy and teachings.

Judaism is another world religion, and it is a monotheistic religion in that its followers recognize and worship only one true God. "It is the oldest monotheistic religion." The Old Testament in the Bible is important to the Judaism religion because they still adhere to the Ten Commandments. God communicated 613 commandments to Moses during the third century CE. The acronym CE means common era. The use of CE in Jewish scholarship was historically motivated by the desire to avoid the implicit of implying that Jesus Christ is Lord. *Amino domini* is the Latin word for the year of the Lord, which was replaced by common era. There are 365 negative commands, corresponding to the number of solar days in a year, and 248 positive commands. The purpose of the commands was to help the Jews function in their daily lives, including family, personal hygiene, and diet. The Ten Commandments are the first ten of the 613 commands of the laws that Judaism follows. Jews believe they are God's chosen people, and they must set an example of right behavior to the world. Everything they do is based upon the Ten Commandments, also known as the Ten Sayings. It is instilled in the hearts of Jews that God gave the Ten Commandments to Moses on two tablets of stone at Mount Sinai. Jesus Christ already came, not to abolish the laws but to fulfill what the laws could not do. Matthew 5:17 (NKJV) states, "Do not think that I came to destroy the Law or the Prophets. I came to fulfill its truth." Judaism's core teachings are about righteousness and justice.

It is estimated 14 million people in the world are Jewish. "About 41% of the Jewish population lives in Israel and 41% lives in the United States, with the remainder concentrated in Europe and North

America" (White, Mary Gormandy, M.A., Staff Writer). Orthodox, conservative, and reform are denominations of the Judaism religion.

Israel has been identified as an important place in the hearts and minds of Jewish people and has historical significance in relationship to their faith.

"The Hebrew Bible, which is also referred to as the *Tanakh,* is the primary holy text of the Jewish faith. It includes the same books as the Old Testament of the Christian Bible, though they are in a different order. The first five books of the Hebrew Bible form the *Torah.*" Another holy text in Judaism is called the *Talmud.* The Talmud entails an in-depth collection of Jewish laws and various teachings of their faith. The Jewish house of worship is called a synagogue. Their ritualistic practices include bat mitzvahs, which are for young girls, while bar mitzvahs are for young boys. Both are equally important in the Jewish faith because they are ceremonies to symbolize when young people have reached adulthood in terms of their responsibilities in their faith.

Looking at the various religions, it can be inferred that Jews acknowledge Jesus as a great teacher. The Hindus know him as a self-realized saint who reached the highest level of consciousness. The Buddhist see him as "bodhisattvas," which means a perfect, enlightened being full of compassion, one who helps people, but do not see him as Christian. The Muslims believe he was born of a virgin just like Christians but see him as a great prophet. They called him "Sabian Marian." The "Sabian's, sometimes also spelled Sabaeans or Sabeans, are a mysterious religious group mentioned three times in the Quran." ("Sabian's"). A reference is made to Jesus as the Son of Mary, though as nothing more than a prophet. [1]"But

---

[1] Apostle Dr. Violet Wallace, 2022 Christmas Service at Faith in Action Deliverance Ministries

I declare today, 12/25/2022, that Jesus Christ is the Savior of the World." Acts 4:12 (NKJV) states, That nor is there salvation in any other, for there is no other name under heaven given among men by which we must be saved. According to 2 Peter 3:9 (NKJV), the Lord is not slack concerning *His* promise, as some count slackness, but is longsuffering toward us, not willing that any should perish but that all should come to repentance.

In contrast to world religions, it should be noted an atheist is a person who does not believe in the existence of God or any other gods. The Greek word for agnostic is agnosticism. Agnosticism means doctrine. An agnostic is a person who believes that nothing is known about the existence of God. Agnostics state that there is no divine.

The Bible commands us to love the Lord with all our heart, but if truth be told, we really do not know how. One would ask how do I love God and I have never seen Him? John 14:9 (NKJV) states, Jesus replied, "Have I been with you all this time, Philip, and yet you still don't know who I am? Anyone who has seen me has seen the Father! So why are you asking me to show him to you?"

The people you see around you, whose lives are in Christ—Jesus is manifesting Himself through them. When we accept Jesus Christ as Savior, Jesus possesses our spirit. Because of the indwelling of the Holy Spirit, greater is He that is in me than he that is in the world. 1 John 4:4 (NKJV) states, But you belong to God, my dear children. You have already won a victory over those people because the spirit who lives in you is greater than the spirit who lives in the world.

There are lot of people that have allowed religion to disrupt the love they have for the Father. Religion destroys our love for God. Religion, through the lens of a noun, has various meanings. Religion can mean the belief in and worship of a superhuman controlling power, especially a personal god or gods. Religion can also be defined as ideas about the relationship between science and religion, a system of faith and worship, or a pursuit or interest to which someone ascribes supreme importance. Yet, religion is difficult to define because human belief structures are varied and complicated. How could I describe religion without highlighting the various disguises of religion and religious behavior in today's world? Religion is a big issue under disguise. Christians declared that Christianity is not a religion, but rather it is a relationship with Jesus Christ. Muslims say Islam is not a religion, but it is a way of life, and Hindus denied they belong to a religion. Paganism, Islam, Buddhism, and Jehovah's Witnesses all believe their religious doctrine are not religion but a way of life.

The formation of a religious sect is known as a religion. European language designates all concepts concerning belief in God, gods, or goddesses as well as other spiritual beings. This is not accepted because they describe religious beliefs but not religion. Religion consists of beliefs, actions, and institutions that assume the existence of the supernatural entities with powers or moral purpose. Some people believe in different deities. For example, I have confidence in Buddha, a female llama. I believe in God, the rabbi affirms. I believe in Jesus Christ, a priest stated. I believe in Allah, a Muslim declares.

We need to love God and serve Him, whether the Pastor leaves or not, fails or not, it is the Lord I love and serve. Love conquers all. Love God "El Ohim," with all your heart. Jesus died to save humanity. When Cain killed Abel, Abel's blood cried out from the ground because man was made from the dust of the ground. Jesus had to die, shed His blood on the cross, and from the cross His blood flows. When the solider pierced Jesus' side, blood and water flowed, the blood of Jesus hit the ground and spoke on behalf of His people. That is why the Word said if you trouble one of His little ones, you might as well put a milestone around your neck and go drown in the sea (Matthew 18:5, NKJV). The Word of God also declares in Hebrew when the blood hit the ground, it runs to the church and tore the veil, meaning it hit the flesh and tore it down and said no flesh shall glory in His presence. James 1:27 (NKJV) speaks of pure and undefiled religion, that is visit the orphans and widows in their trouble and to keep one unspotted from the world. Any form of worship that exalts other gods or ideologies other than Jesus Christ as the only way to the Father is a false religion. Jesus Christ is the way, the truth, and the life, and the only way to the Father is through the son. (John 14:6 New Living Translation). One must have a relationship with Jesus Christ.

Mercy represents shed blood. God reigns in holiness and holiness means to be set apart. There is tension between faith and religion. One that you see play out over and over again throughout the Bible with the prophets saying that God does not want your sacrifices and burnt offerings. God wants your steadfast love, he wants your complete commitment, and a servitude spirit. Jesus Christ battled with the spirit of religion when He encountered the Pharisees and the Sadducees, who were purveyors of religion. Jesus Christ died while religion was still spreading worldwide. People believed religion over a relationship with the Savior Jesus Christ. Religion does not save, and religion does not give life. Only the Lord Jesus Christ and a relationship with Him does. Religion is an idea. The spreader of religion is of traditional value. Religion is a set of beliefs, feelings, dogmas, and practices that define the relationship between human beings.

The word religion is derived from the Latin word *religio*. Religion has many gods because the heaven and the earth contain many diverse parts. Many gods exist because the gods are the cosmos and can be manipulated, and also because humans are obsessed with sex, money, and self. The universe is unified as the creation of the one true God "El Ohim." He alone is God. He should not be compared to any common denomination god. God is completely separated from all other gods. The almighty God cannot be manipulated through the cosmos of any other gods because He is not the cosmos. God created the world as a universe within His own unified purpose of it. Human beings are designed not to appease capricious and power-hungry gods but to worship and obey the true and living Creator. The ultimate security and peace come from trusting and worshipping the Creator. "True Christianity is to oppose all forms of mysticism. Therefore, we cannot separate our experience from the Word of God. Some examples are a real birth at Bethlehem. A real death at Calvary. A real Savior Christ. A real resurrection in the garden tomb and real ascension at the Mount of Olives. Every other truth in the Bible in some way or another supports that message. So, Acts 1:9-12, KJV indicates, sinners that come to believe in this Christ are saved, holy, adopted and loved by God and in turn love God. (1 John 5:1-10, Ephesians 2:1-9)" Schortmann, 2020, p. 6.

How it all Began

A religious Babylonian system is where it all began. The Babylonians were a sect that expressed hostility toward God. Babylon stems from the Tower of Babel. According to Genesis 11:1-10 (NLT), people spoke the same language. Before the world was split, separated, and scattered, God had to confuse the people because they found a plain in the land of Babylon and said let's make brick and harden them with fire bricks, which were used instead of stone. Tar was used for mortar. The Tower of Babel was orchestrated by Nimrod, the son of Cush and great-grandson of Noah. The Babylonians wanted to build a tower to reach heaven as to make them famous and to keep the people from being scattered all over the world. The people were united and set out to build the Tower of Babel; however, God caused them to speak in different tongues. God did that for a purpose; that's why you cannot listen to other voices because it brings confusion. The Lord scattered them all over the world. That is how the Lord confused the world with different languages. Babel means confusion in the land of Babylon.

The Babylonians rejection toward God caused God to kill off everybody except Noah and his family. God did not allow Noah to open the door to the ark because the people were rebellious. Babylon was later the capital that cruelly conquered Judah, fought them, and captured them. That is how Daniel and his friends were captured, the foe of the enemy of God's people. The essence and its application to the world in which we live in today is the great Babylon. Revelation 18:2 (NKJV) states, And he cried mightily with a loud voice, saying, "Babylon the great is fallen, and has become a dwelling place of demons, a prison for every foul spirit, and a cage for every unclean and hated bird!" The lasting type of carnality is greed, and it all comes from Babylon. The people were greedy, they wanted everything for themselves; they were cruel leaders, and because God's people survived, they sought to destroy them. Babylon was to the Jews the essence of cruelty against God's people.

Religious Babylon is the System
Do not be swayed by the religious world system. We are Christians, and we do not follow their patterns. Babylon came into being long

before Christianity. It is satanic. The Babylonian system is satanic because it imitated God and because they had previous knowledge of how God's system operated. They anticipated the coming of the true Messiah called Jesus. Semiramis, an idol worshipper, had a miracle boy named Tammuz, and he was considered to be a savior. However, the real Messiah came, (Jesus Christ of Nazareth), and it resulted in the reason why there is war against the true church, even in the current dispensation we are living in. They did not believe Jesus Christ is Lord and Savior; that is why they killed him. Tammuz is not Jesus. Ezekiel 8:14 (NLT) states, They were weeping for Tammuz because he died. While the war wages on against the true church, we thank God that Jesus Christ was resurrected and is on the throne at the right hand of God, interceding on behalf of those whom God the Father has given to him.

Universal Religion

Babylon sits on many waters. It is a universal international character and can be attributed to universal religion. Universal religion is called false religion. The woman in Revelation 17 (NKJV) represents false religion that will dominate the world in the tribulation period. The tribulation period is known as the Day of the Lord. False religion is not limited to any church as some would believe. Many believe it is the Roman Catholic church is the universal church. However, it is more than that. It is a religious spirit over the nation that can come through Buddhism or any sector. It is not limited to the Roman Catholic church. It is far beyond that.

Chapter 2
RELATIONSHIP

When it comes to having a relationship with God, it must be noted there is no such thing as church online. The "devil is a liar" because when you go to church online you cannot get baptized online, a baby cannot get christened online, and you cannot go and visit a person who is hospitalized from attending church online. The system of this world is not the system of our God and it is designed to keep us in bondage. The Bible says do not forsake assembling with yourself and believers and that is where the anointing comes from—fellowship. It is a relationship and a fellowship (Apostle Dr. Violet Wallace 12/31/2022, New Year's Eve Service). Hebrews 10:25 (NKJV) states, not forsaking the assembling of ourselves together, as *is* the manner of some, but exhorting *one another,* and so much the more as you see the Day approaching.

For this is how God loved the world: He gave his one and only son so that everyone who believes in him will not perish but have eternal life (John 3:16 NLT). Life is lived in relationships. Some are deep rooted, and others are superficial. Some are of short duration, others last a lifetime, some are purely functional, others are intense and personal. A religion that does not permeate daily life is dead and meaningless. Living a spiritual life is being fruitful in all areas of righteousness. Religion is one who is outwardly. Is your love greater than your hurt? It is hurt that hinders, and it is a plan of the devil. We need to get over all the hurt. Get your mind connected to God so you do not leave the same way you came. When you love the Lord, you will work for the Lord in obedience and submission and you will have a relationship with Him.

Love is fierce, it has the characteristic of death (Romans 8:37 NLT). Love is a conqueror. When love grabs you, it will not let you go. Love is stronger than your will. Love cannot be controlled by man, especially the agape love. Let love control you. Guard your heart, and do not play with love. Jesus is love. 1 John 4:16 (NKJV), stated, and we have known and believed the love that God has for us. God is love, and he who abides in love abides in God, and God in him. Do not wake love until you are ready to please it. Love is a healer to all wounds. Love causes Jesus to die and conquer death. It was love that got Christ Jesus up, it was love that caused Him to endure. Love can overcome your vows and commitment to a common god. Be careful, love is a consuming fire. God is love. Many people love today, but not tomorrow.

Lust is the lowest part of love. Love can pull you to something wrong. We can do something in the name of love and its wrong. It is the trick of the enemy. The reason why some of us are struggling is because we love ourselves more than God. Romans 1:26-32 (Amplified Bible).

Be careful and guard your heart. Proverbs 1:23 (NKJV) states, Because out of it flows the issues of life. Issues here means desires. The desires of this life will cause you to reject God and turn away from Him. The devil works in the flow of love. People say they love their spouse and displease God. The devil causes hurt through love. So sometimes we say I do not want to be vulnerable and get hurt. I am dropping my guard because I do not want to get hurt by false love, God's love is genuine. Love can get perverted when it flows through lust. True love must flow through God's love alone. The person that loves the Lord with all their heart will love you for real, their love will be genuine. Whatever the greatest love is, it will control everything under it.

Some of us love our hurt more than God and that is why we cling to it and will not let it go. We use the hurt to look for legal excuses to demonstrate the hurt, but God wants to take away the excuses of hurt that's hindering you. Let God be the greatest love in your life. "I love you Lord and I lift my voice to worship you." Some people struggle to submit to the love of God because of the pain they feel. God's love is able to deliver you and save you. Many have the excuse that there is no love in the church, but it is God who erects the church in love. So what they say is based on their personal experience with an individual and attribute to church hurt, not the body of Christ. The church is a body, not an individual. Is your love greater than your hurt? When your love is greater, it loves all hurt, it heals, it subjects, if forgets. 1 Corinthians 13:1-7 (NLT) states, "If I could speak all the languages of earth and of angels, but didn't love others, I would only be a noisy gong or a clanging cymbal. If I had the gift of prophecy, and if I understood all of God's secret plans and possessed all knowledge, and if I had such faith that I could move mountains, but didn't love others, I would be nothing. If I gave everything I have to the poor and even sacrificed my body, I could boast about it; but if I didn't love others, I would have gained nothing. Love is patient and kind. Love is not jealous or boastful or proud or rude. It does not demand its own way. It is not irritable, and it keeps no record of being wronged. It does not rejoice about injustice but rejoices whenever the truth wins out. Love never gives up, never loses faith, is always hopeful, and endures through every circumstance." It is hurt that hinders and it is a plan of the devil. We need to get over all the hurt but can only get over it through the power of love. The power of love comes from a true connection with God. When you love the Lord, you will work for love. You will suffer because of love; you will endure to love. When you love the Lord, you will quench any fiery darts with love. Acts 2 (NKJV) states, Because God is love, He is in the church. Where is love? Love is God who lives in the heart of humans who submit to Him. Where is religion? Religion is in the mind and heart. Some people love tradition and not truth. Some people love religion more than the true God and people. Love overcomes tradition and religion. When people love something, they find a way to keep it, but when it comes onto God, their loves can't seem to find a way to live for Him, spend time with Him or give Him their all.

When you love God, you will step out of your comfort zone. Your hurt can be so deep that you reject God and His people. Hurt will cause you to reject the love of God. Hurt will cause you to reject the church of God. As believers, if we are not careful, we can easily be involved in religion and be oblivious of it. Religion can easily dominate your prayer life and dominate your walk with Jesus Christ. Religion can cripple your relationship with God. Believers can use religious excuse to live in rebellion and worldliness. Religion is very different from a relationship with God through Jesus Christ. Religions are manmade and are based on rules, regulations and good work. Religion is based on human effort. Relationship is based on living and obeying the Word of God. When I look in the Old and the New Testaments, serving God is not based on human effort, but on love and commitment to Jesus Christ as Lord and Savior. Religion's goals are to do good or right and work our way into heaven. Religion says if I give to charity, I will earn my way into heaven. Religion says I did nothing wrong I am a good person. Religion says I read my Bible, and I go to church, but that is not enough. When you have a relationship with God our goals are to fully trust Him, live to please Him and confess our sins. It also involves being sorrowful of wrongdoing, receiving the Holy Spirit, and allowing Him to control your lives. The relationship we have with Jesus Christ will result in joy, peace, freedom, victory, power, and eternal life with Him in heaven. God's way to restore man back to Him is Jesus because the relationship was broken. Religion is the belief in a God or a group of Gods. Religion is an interest, a belief, or an activity that is very important to a person or group. We serve Jesus Christ not because we think we must, but because we want to. Acts 4:12 (NKJV) said, there is no salvation in no other but the one Christ Jesus. Who earn His name among every other name by which man must be saved? There are many types of religions, but there is only one Lord and Savior, Jesus Christ. There are many types of religions in our world, but they cannot save you from your sins. There are many different religions, why say religion! Because their God is dead and was never raised. Their god's bones are still in the grave. But Jesus got up. There are many types of religion, but their powers are futile. There are many types of religion, but I came to find out, they cannot heal you. They cannot work miracles. There are many types of religions, but they cannot provide for you. There are many types of religions, but they cannot keep you alive by blowing breath in you. Seek for the relationship that was once broken by sin. Do not seek religion.

We must be delivered from demonic deception, religious deception, and self-deception. We need to be free from world religions. Free masonry is a religious demonic deception. John 18:20 (NKJV) states, no secret society should be plain to the naked eye. We need to be rescued from homosexuality and cultic practices. Religious deception is deceitful. Matthew 4:7 (NKJV) said believe not every spirit but test every spirit whether they be of God or not. Supernatural gifts and miracles of healing do not guarantee the genuine real work; rather, a real work shows and manifest Jesus as Savior. Jesus does not use His power for vain glory. People must be saved and then they will see miracles. Paul said in the Book of Romans that you must walk in the spirit so that you will not fulfill the lust of the flesh. We must be delivered from deception of all kinds. We must be delivered from sorcery and witchcraft of all kinds. 1 Samuel 15 (NKJV) states that disobedience is a form of witchcraft. Negative speech, manipulation, and mind control is a form of witchcraft. Be delivered from end time mind control. Be delivered from the spirit of alcohol. Yes, being addicted to alcohol is a spirit of Satan, and it comes from your own desire and family lineage. Be delivered from demons affects the family, causing spiritual disorder. Remember Jezebel and Ahab. Be delivered from demons affecting the body such as sleeplessness, hangovers, nervous stomach, red eye, headache, hypoglycemia, physical illnesses, and infirmities etc.

Chapter 3
THE ESCHATOLOGY

Many people do not read the Book of Revelation because of the way in which it was written. 2 Timothy 3:16-17 (AMP) states all Scripture is God-breathed given by divine inspiration and is profitable for instruction, for conviction [of sin], for correction [of error and restoration to obedience], for training in righteousness [learning to live in conformity to God's will, both publicly and privately—behaving honorably with personal integrity and moral courage]; so that the man of God may be complete *and* proficient, outfitted *and* thoroughly equipped for every good work.

The Book of Revelation was written to the seven churches. It was not written for us to be fearful or for us to feel doomed. The Book of Revelation was written to the seven churches for their edification and to let them know what time and dispensation we are living in. It is an apocalyptic (end times) book. A person who reads and studies the Book of Revelation must also read and study the Book of Daniel because they both contain visions and coincide with each other. In studying the Book of Revelation and through spiritual insight and Godly wisdom, a person will learn when they read about the ten horns, locusts, and scorpions, that the Book of Revelation's content is written prophetically, literally, and figuratively.

Where sin is concerned, 2 Corinthians 5:10 (NKJV) states, for we must all appear before the judgment seat of Christ, that each one may receive the things done in the body, according to what he has done, whether good or bad. Believers will face a day of judgement. The white throne of judgment is for the non-believers, and the judgement throne is for the believers. 1 John 1:8 (NKJV) states, if we say that we have no sin, we deceive ourselves, and the truth is not in us. True believers will not sin habitually as a way of life. Christians sin, Christians are not sinners. New life in Christ means a born-again Christian must live sinlessness. Our new nature cannot and will not sin. If we practice this, we will walk more in spiritual perfection. If we practice living life in Christ, governed by the indwelling of the Holy Spirit, it will become a habit that we not sin habitually. 1 John 3:8-9 (NKJV) states, He who sins is of the devil, for the devil has sinned from the beginning. For this purpose, the Son of God was manifested, that He might destroy the works of the devil. Whoever has been born of God does not sin, for His seed remains in him; and he cannot sin, because he has been born of God. In our new nature, born again, sanctified and set apart, Romans 6:6 (NKJV) states, knowing this, that our old man was crucified with Him, that the body of sin might be done away with, that we should no longer be slaves of sin. The more we yield to the *Holy Spirit, it is to the true revelation of God.* 1 Corinthians 10:13 (NKJV) laments, No temptation has overtaken you except such as is common to man; but God is faithful, who will not allow you to be tempted beyond what you are able, but with the temptation will also make the way of escape, that you may be able to bear it.

When Jesus returns, He is looking for himself in you, that your garments not be soiled, and that you are a church without spot or wrinkles. The church is not a physical building, but it is the body of Christ. Life eternally, is in a relationship with Jesus Christ. The world in which we live in and know is only temporal. 1 Corinthians 7:31 (NLT) states those who use the things of the world should not become attached to them. For this world as we know it will soon pass away. Are you ready to go? If you do not go, are you ready for His return? You must go if he does not return and when he returns in the rapture, you must go. What do you know about the end times and spiritual insight about the Book of Revelation? Acknowledge that the Book of Revelation has been scribed literally, figuratively, and symbolically as well as prophetically; the Book of Revelation is not religiosity, but it will help you to understand the apocalyptic times of where one can end up if they do not have a relationship with Jesus Christ, have a form of godliness, or they are just living and existing in this world. The first death is when you do not have a relationship with Christ. "Natural man cannot receive the truth of God's word. Natural man is dead in his sins and trespasses and at enmity with God. (Romans 8:7; 1 Corinthians 2:10-6; 2 Corinthians 2:14-17; Ephesians 2:1-9). Sin has consequences, and as a result, man left to himself does not believe in the true God or in His word or in His Christ. When we are born again by the Holy Spirit, giving the gift of faith in Jesus, our eyes and mind and heart are open to the truth of Christ and we believe. The truth of God has set us free" (Schormann 2020, p. 8). Revelation unveils the mystery of God's plan. Written by Apostle John on the Island of Patmos, while in the spirit, not the flesh. The flesh must be specified because the flesh is attributed to earthly wisdom and composed of humans' five senses. In the flesh, one will never be able to comprehend the spirit because supernatural events are only spiritually discerned. 1 Corinthians 2:14 (NKJV) states, But the natural man does not receive the things of the Spirit of God, for they are foolishness to him; nor can he know them, because they are spiritually discerned. Apostle John was in exile after having been beaten by the Roman soldiers and left to die on the Island of Patmos when the holy spirit gave him the revelation knowledge to scribe what we know today to be the Book of Revelation. There are seven lamps of fire that symbolically equate to the seven spirits of God. Wisdom, knowledge an understanding is a part of the Godly wisdom, and when one has them bestowed upon them, they think like God, act like God, look like God, and behave like God. It is not to be construed with or thinking that one is God or is a God; it's simply indicative of the characteristics that one must possess as a believer to live a life in Christ.

Revelation 17:4 (NKJV) speaks of the woman who was arrayed in purple and gold with precious stones, which symbolize a fight for power. One of the ecclesiastics' corruption is the lust for temporal power. The scarlet represents rulers; that is why they are looking at the Roman Catholic, but that is where they are fooled. We, who are the body of Christ, are not guessing because in Matthew 7:15-20 (NKJV) it explains that by their fruit, we will know them. That is the reason why in the Book of Daniel, they could not fool Daniel into worshipping their idols. Matthew 24:37 (NKJV) states, "As it was in the days of Noah, so will it be at the coming of the Son of Man." The Book of Revelation speaks of the seven heads and twelve horns with blasphemed against God written all over it. The woman was holding a goblet with her obscenities. Who is the woman and what is the symbolic meaning of the woman? First, the goblet with her obscenities represents, impurities, cursing and using foul language, the world of gay lifestyle, kinky sex, mother of prostitutes, and sexual immorality. The woman is sitting in a temporal world in a position on a scarlet beast. The woman literally represents the kings of the earthly world, the world leaders in their authority and powers.

Chapter 4

WHERE IS YOUR RELATIONSHIP WITH JESUS CHRIST?

The Word of God tells us that greater is He that is in us than he that is the world. We are given a command to hide the Word of God in our heart that we may not sin against Him. As well as those who are in the world, being an enemy of God. We must have a relationship with Jesus Christ and not be unevenly yoked. We cannot serve two masters because we will love one or the other or hate one or the other. Idols are anything that we put before God, and nothing else matters.

It's imperative to ascertain where your relationship is with Jesus Christ. The systems of this world are not the systems of our God. The systems could be used for good and evil. Either building up the kingdom of God or enlarging hell's mouth. Is Jesus Christ prioritized in your life through an intimate relationship or has everything else been put before Him? 2 Corinthians 11:2 (The Message Bible) states, Will you put up with a little foolish aside from me? Please, just for a moment. The thing that has me so upset is that I care about you so much—this is the passion of God burning inside me! I promised your hand in marriage to Christ, presented you as a pure virgin to her husband. And now I'm afraid that exactly as the snake seduced Eve with his smooth tongue, you are being lured away from the simple purity of your life for Christ.

[2]INSTITUTIONS OF THE WORLD SYSTEM

These institutions are listed in the likely biblical order of importance and are contrasted with how it probably is in the United States of America.

Cultural Shapers of Values (for good or evil) Below is the likely Biblical order of importance	USA's Order
1. Religion (the church): **Exodus 20:3-6; Matt. 22:36-40** (Exists to represent the God of the Bible, evangelize, disciple, restrain evil, and influence the world. The church is in the world but operates within a Biblical worldview)	5th
2. The Family Unit (Society): **Matt. 19-4-6; Eph. 5:21-33** Consists of the marriage of one man and one woman. Exists to populate the earth, love, nurture, and teach their children A. Educational/Academic System (Worldviews) • Primary schooling (K-4) • Secondary (5-12) • Postgraduate (college)	4th 2nd

---

2 By permission Skeba, D., 2006, The Armor of God: Winning the Invisible War

3. Civil Government: Romans 13:1-7; Genesis 9:6 A. <u>Political Systems</u>: (America's are **bolded**) • *Theocracy*—rule by God (i.e. Israel under the Mosaic law prior to their kings) • *Monarchy*—rule by one (i.e. Saddam Hussein in Iraq; Emperor worship in Japan) • *Oligarchy*—rule by a few elite (The USSR) • *Democracy*—rule by majority • ***Republic*-rule by law** (U.S.A*) **Executive Branch** (law enforcement body) **Legislative Branch** (lawmaking body) **Judicial Branch** (legal body) • *Anarchy*-rule by none (a temporary stage) • Though founded as a republic, there is good reason to believe it not to be an oligarchy. B. <u>Economic Systems</u>: (The Business Sector including Technology & Commercial Industry): • **Free Enterprise (called Capitalism)** • Fascism (private ownership with gov't control) • Socialism (government owns the property and controls the production)	1st
4. The Communications Media (via TV/radio/internet/print publications/music) • Arts and Entertainment Industry • The News	3rd

The nation has gone off the path that God has set for the people. The path starts from one's family life and home. As a result of having gone off the path that God has set for the people, here comes the judgement, here comes the war, global warming, tsunamis, floods, and fires.

The political, economic, and religious systems are the ultimate problem for destruction of the nation. The people on the earth are disobedient. We want to do our own things, wear our pants down, pierce our skin. Do not sleep with anybody until you are married. The political system establishes justice and obedience to God. That is why in the courthouse, you see trust in God, which they removed eventually (Deuteronomy 16:18-20). The economic system is for stewardship. One must give generously (Deuteronomy 6:10; 15:1-18). The religious system is supposed to bring people into a relationship with God and to ground the political and economic systems in God. What is happening is that instead of the religious system bringing the world into God, people are falling away from God and living solely by the political and governmental and economic systems. The church is supposed to bring them and keep them in God. That is why God is saying pray, because the systems are out of line, and it is causing judgment in the earth. The religious system provides a fence for the community and gives them life. That is why we get out of bondage. The church and the state cannot mix and do not go together because the church must be the governing body that keeps the political and economic systems in place. When the religious system gets out of order, everything else is up for grabs and becomes a foot hole for the enemy to come in. When the rich and the poor are segregated, it shows that people and the nation are far from God. We are not supposed to be segregated because the rich are supposed to help the poor and the poor are supposed to help the rich. There is reciprocity.

Which Church are You?
The church is not an individual, groups that compound cliques, or a building location. The church is the body of Christ.

The church that we are in will give us a reference to whom our relationship is with. In Apostle's John's diction to the seven churches in the Book of Revelation, the church of Ephesus is depicted as a loveless church, rejected and evil, and it must do its first work over to receive the crown of life. Located in Corinth, the church of Smyrna is described as one who gratefully bear suffering, they were the persecuted church and were told be faithful unto so they can receive the crown of life. James 1:12 (NKJV) states, Blessed *is* the man who endures temptation; for when he has been approved, he will receive the crown of life which the Lord has promised to those who love Him. The church of Pergamos was in Galatians and it was the compromising church. The church of Thyatira was in Ephesians, and it was a church that displayed, love, service, patients, and faith. The ought against it was that it tolerated the occult and immorality. The Jezebel spirit was present. Such a spirit possesses pastors of the church, whether male or female. Thyatira was a corrupt church. The Jezebel spirit is not only about a woman sleeping with a married man. It is a controlling and manipulating spirit that must not be allowed to manifest in the church because the people will be led astray. We see this today in some churches. It helps us to understand that nothing is new, the time is different, but Ecclesiastes 1:9, NKJV, states, that which has been is what will be, that which is done is what will be done, and there is nothing new under the sun. The church of Sardis in Philippi is considered the dead church. People have left there and are struggling to live for Christ. The church is alive in the world but dead in the things that pertain to God. They must get themselves together and stop being busy in the world. They must repent and strengthen what remains. God promised faithfulness and honor and to put a white garment on them like He is wearing. The church of Philadelphia was the church that operated in faith. They kept the Word of Christ and honored His Word. God did not have any criticism about them. They did not spoil their garments. They keep the faith, overcome testing and trials. They will have a place in God's presence, a new name, and a new Jerusalem in heaven, not the one on Earth. The church of Laodicea in Thessalonians was zealous and always repenting. But they were indifferent in that they were neither hot or cold, but just a lukewarm church. It pays to be faithful, it pays to be loyal, it pays to stand on the truth and live by the Word of God. God promised to keep the believer from tribulation. This oath is meant for God to protect them during trials, judgement, and tribulation. Always be ready for Jesus coming!

Chapter 5
BEFORE IT'S TOO LATE

We as born-again believers must do what Christ did before he ascended. Christ's commission helps us to understand that we must "go into all the world and preach the gospel to all creation. He who has believed and has been baptized will be saved; but he who has disbelieved shall be condemned." These signs will accompany those who have believed: in My name they will cast out demons, they will speak with new tongues; they will pick up serpents, and if they drink any poison, will not hurt them; they will lay hands on the sick, and they will recover" (Mark 16:15-18 NKJV). Repent, get baptized, live by faith, and receive the "sacred and imperishable proclamation of eternal salvation" (Schortmann, 2020).

Have confidence in life in Him. We who have the Word of God have the power to know we have life. Everybody uses life; the Word of God is not written to those who are outside of God, but it is written to those who have God. One can only speak of life when they have the spirit of God in them.

Jesus said not my will, your will, God, be done (Mark 14:36 NLKJV). Jesus faced his trepidation over the upcoming suffering he would endure on the cross by praying for strength to do his Father's will. Man is a spirit living in a body, which has a soul. The Spirit of God makes the soul come alive in the body, and the soul is quickening the body because the soul commits to the spirit and gave credence of place for the nudging to the body.

If we were quickened by the Spirit of God, He quickens our soul, thus causing us to move.

The indwelling of the holy spirit causes your spirit to make known to you; you have another entity in you. Who is in us? It is the Spirit of God? The Spirit of God is the will of God.

Jesus said, Not my will, but your will be done. It is your will that cause me to breathe, to act, and to move. It is your will to be made alive in you. So, my will submits to the will of God.

My will that is being made alive has now recognized the spirit in me, which is the will.

When I submit my will, my emotions obey, talk with Him, listen to Him, be obedient to Him, I automatically come into spiritual alignment through a sanctification, holy living, and a righteous lifestyle.

God's will is Himself in you. Our will becomes one with Him to move us to the higher heights, deeper depths, favor; because it's all HIM that we submit to.

So, His will is the Word too. God made flesh and His Word is the creation. His Word is my healing.

It is His will, you, which is the Spirit of God. Without His will, which is Himself, you would not have the spirit, which entails spiritual deeper depths and higher heights. Jesus overcame because He submitted to the Father. Jesus said I do what the Father says.

If we submit our will, meaning I am not going to do that because He is in me, and I am Him.

Jesus said it is my Father's will to give you the kingdom, to give Him of yourself. It is your will for you to submit and take Him at

His will so God's purpose, plan, desire, His will be done—who you submit to.

Christ is God. Who are we? We are God, his servants. That is why whatever he says through us is law, it goes, and it is whatever we manifest.

Jeremiah 29:11 (NKJV) states, That it is Him. He knows what He has for you, but the plan is his, not ours. It becomes what He wants to do and what He requires of us.

Command He me, if it is Gods will for anything, He is going to do it. At Faith in Action Deliverance Ministries, He is the one who has the blue print, the one who you are; anyone who knows the blue print is who you are going to ask permission and get it from to do things. His will is Himself that dwelleth in you and you submit to, and you have confidence in who lives in you.

If people do not have life in Christ, they are dead because He is the life. John 14:16 (NKJV) states, Jesus saith unto him, I am the way, the truth, and the life: no man cometh unto the Father, but by me.

Jesus Christ is God's son, and Jesus could not give God to anybody himself. Jesus had to ask God. Father they have been asking me, to give me you, but I cannot give them you. I am asking you if you could give them what you have gave me, which is your will. Your will is to set me free. Jesus said can you send your will back to them. The Father said, If they do what I do. Jesus told them to go to the upper room. So, those who accept Jesus Christ, he could also give his will freely to; those, after having died on the cross of Calvary more than two thousand years ago. It is not your will to do what you want to do; it is the Father's will to do what He wants you to do, and that is what you must do.

Temptation comes from evil desires inside us, not from God. It begins with a sinful thought and we allow it to affect our behavior. Sin grows more destructive the more we let it have its way. Live a sin-free life daily. We have no more excuses, and there is no more sacrifice for sin. We must live a perfect life in God. Luke 19:10 (NLT) states, For the Son of Man came to seek and save those who are lost. 2 Peter 3:8-10 (NLT) states but you must not forget this one thing, dear friends: A day is like a thousand years to the Lord, and a thousand years is like a day. The Lord isn't really being slow about his promise as some people think. No, he is being patient for your sake. He does not want anyone to be destroyed but wants everyone to repent. But the day of the Lord will come as unexpectedly as a thief. Then the heavens will pass away with a terrible noise, and the very elements themselves will disappear in fire, and the earth and everything on it will be found to deserve judgment.

In the end time from the beginning of time, there is tribulation, so the world is not going to be easy (Ecclesiastics 1:9). That is the reason we have Christ and we must have a relationship with him. In Acts 14:22 (NLT), you will see that was a great tribulation. In the Book of Daniel, the tribulation gets intensified. The Bible said it's going to be so severe because of sin. The more sin increases, the greater judgment and tribulation. The more sin increases, the greater the trial. Sin cuts the human lifestyle. Evil is always present, but we must endure till the end. By keeping our robe white and staying under the blood, you will endure. Matthew 24:13 (NKJV) states, But he who endures to the end shall be saved.

No one can come to God unless the indwelling of the holy spirit invites them. You do not decide that on your own. If the holy spirit invites you, it means the holy spirit has convicted you; that is why you have a conscience. Sin entered and caused a separation from

God. Sin had to be purged from heaven and it must also be purged from the earth. The Kingdom of God is at hand. When you see all these things happening in the world, Luke 21:28 (NIV) states, When these things begin to take place, stand up and lift your heads because your redemption is drawing near. There is no repentance from the grave. When you die, the body goes back to the ground, your soul, which is your mind, will, and emotions goes to either a place of rest or torment, and your spirit, if there is no sin, will return to God. Repent and turn from yours sins. Become born again, according to John 3:1-10 (NLT). The only way to the Father is through the Son. Ensure you have a relationship with Jesus Christ and do not just exist and practice a religion. Come nearer to God so that He may come nearer to you. There are five ways to come near to God. One, submit to God. Two, yield to him that he will be in your life and commit your life to him. Three, lead a pure life (wash your hands). Four, grieve, mourn, and wail in sincere sorrow for your sins. Five, you must humble yourself before the Lord, and he will lift you up.

What sorrow awaits those whose pride causes them to fall? Pride comes before a fall, and it leads to death. We may think we are in the house of safety, but our sin will surely find us out as judgement first begins in the house of God. When we think it's peace and safety, its sudden destruction. No one is exempt. You cannot use God as a fire extinguisher. Abusing your privileges is vain confidence. Everyone will be judged according to their works because many people say they are living in God but living in sin and in conformity to the world. So, everyone that exalts themselves shall be abased. Pride goes before a fall and we should not get comfortable with material blessings because they are only temporary and should be used for God's glory, not for our self-gratification. For what a man sows, that shall he also reap.

Ask oneself these questions, "I wonder what we think about life? Why we have life? Why we were born? And especially why we were born again to Christ or in Christ? And I wonder what we think about the world? What is it? What about the people? Who are they? What are they? And where are they going? The Lord of the Harvest has called us to Himself. He sent workers out into the field and he will reap a wonderful harvest of souls one day, all to His glory, and to our joy in His glory.

SUMMARY

A cult is "a group of people with extreme dedication to a certain leader or set of beliefs that are often viewed as odd by others." Whether they be a cult, religious practices, rituals, and worship of idols, anything other than a relationship with Jesus Christ will lead a person astray.

Although there are different religions, the "Biblical Christian faith is an evangelical religion" (Schortmann, 2020, p. 16). 1 Peter 3:15-17 indicates to tell people about Jesus. The harvest is ready and the laborers are few. Christ sends his workers into the vineyard so that we may tell people about the Gospel of Jesus Christ if they ask and even when they do not ask. Jesus Christ must be ministered to everyone. The Apostle Paul states it best in 1 Corinthians 9:18-23 (NKJV), What is my reward then? That when I preach the gospel, I may present the gospel of Christ without charge, that I may not abuse my authority in the gospel. For though I am free from all men, I have made myself a servant to all, that I might win the more; and to the Jews I became as a Jew, that I might win Jews; to those who are under the law, as under the law, that I might win those who are under the law; to those who are without law, as without law (not being without law toward God, but under law toward Christ), that I might win those who are without law; to the weak I became as weak, that I might win the weak. I have become all things to all men, that I might save some. Now this I do for the gospel's sake, that I may be partaker of it with you. "Once a man or a woman receives the Light and the Life and the love of Christ, we cannot keep Him to ourselves. Christ in us comes out of us" (Galatians 2:20) (Schortmann, 2020, p. 17). Every human being has an eternal soul. Eternity is spent in one place or another. One place it can be spent is suffering under God's offended justice as God's enemies. Another place it can be spent is by rejoicing in the love and friendship of God as His beloved children reconciled in Christ. This will happen if an individual either rejects or receives the Gospel of Jesus Christ that is ministered unto them.

According to Revelation 19, its time we prep ourselves to go to the wedding. The last final invitation was given, and the preparation was made for those that have their RSVPs. There was a count, so God had to invite us to come, our rejection of the invitation resulted in our name not being in the book of life. What will you do to have eternal life? Stop being human and be a spiritual being. The spiritual seeks spiritual satisfaction! The spirit is what grants you access because "I see myself in you, so you are one of mine." Partake in what quickens your spirit, which is a relationship with Jesus Christ. Do not be stubborn, leaning to your own understanding, when it should be God's, for Proverbs 3:5-6 (NKJV) states, Trust in the Lord with all your heart; do not depend on your own understanding. Seek his will in all you do, and he will show you which path to take. Choose Jesus Christ today and decide to have a relationship with Him.

VOCABULARY

1. Intimacy: is defined as a close familiarity or friendship; closeness. Intimacy refers to a level of closeness where you feel validated and safe.

2. Bodhisattvas: one whose goal is awakening in Buddhism; one who seeks awakening, hence, an individual on the path to becoming a buddha.

3. Babel: is a city in Shinar where the building of a tower is held in Genesis to have been halted by the confusion of tongues. It is also a confusion of sounds or voices and a scene of noise or confusion.

4. Burka: a burqa or a burka is an enveloping outer garment worn by women which fully covers the body and the face in some Islamic traditions. Also known as a chadaree or chaadar in Pakistan, Afghanistan, and Iran, or a paranja in Central Asia. The Arab version of the burqa is called the boshiya and is usually black.

5. Figuratively: is an adverb of the adjective figurative that means "of the nature of or involving a figure of speech." It's typically metaphorical and not literal, which is a key difference in common usage between figuratively and literally.

6. Karma: is the force generated by a person's actions held in Hinduism and Buddhism to perpetuate transmigration and in its ethical consequences to determine the nature of the person's next existence.

7. Literally: is an adverb and means "actually," and we use it when we want others to know we're serious, not exaggerating or being metaphorical.

8. Caliphate: an Islamic state, especially one ruled by a single religious and political leader.

9. Caliphs: in Islamic history, the ruler of the Muslim community.

10. Desires: is a longing or craving, as for something that brings satisfaction or enjoyment.

11. Eschatology: refers to the end of the world or end times. It is predicted by several world religions (both Abrahamic and non-Abrahamic), which teach that negative world events will reach a climax. The term refers metaphorically to the end of ordinary reality and to reunion with the divine.

12. Hijab: the Quran instructs Muslim women and men to dress modestly, and for some, the hijab is worn by Muslim girls and women to maintain modesty and privacy from unrelated males. According to the *Encyclopedia of Islam and Muslim World*, modesty concerns both men's and women's "gaze, gait, garments, and genitalia."

13: Metaphorically: a figure of speech that refers to one thing in terms of another, suggesting a resemblance between the two.

14. Monk: a monk is a man who has dedicated his live to religion, partly by giving up some aspects of regular, worldly life. Many monks live together in a religious community. To a greater or lesser extent, a monk has chosen to leave society and devote his life to prayer and service.

15. Niqab: is the Arabic term for veils that cover the whole of the body including the hair, neck, shoulders, and face, except eyes and hands. Through Niqab some people simply wish to be identified as Muslims. They say that wearing Niqab gives them a sense of freedom and liberation for choosing personal attire and clothing.

16. Philosophy: quite literally, the term "philosophy" means, "love of wisdom." In a broad sense, philosophy is an activity people undertake when they seek to understand fundamental truths about themselves, the world in which they live, and their relationships to the world and to each other.

17: Prophetically: of, relating to, or characteristic of a prophet or prophecy; foretelling events, predictive.

18. Ramadan: is a holy month of worship, study of the Quran, prayer, and fasting. Ramadan occurs during the month in which Muslims believe the Quran began to be revealed to the Prophet Muhammad. It is a celebration for Muslims. Fasting is one of the Five Pillars of Islam

19. Sabians: are a mysterious religious group mentioned three times in the Quran.

20. Sharia Law: is a term that refers to a set of Islamic religious law that governs aspects of day-to-day life for Muslims in addition to religious rituals. Sharia law also provides religious followers with a set of principles and guidelines to help them make important decisions in their lives such as finances and investments. It is derived from the Quran, Islam's holy book, as well as the Sunnah and Hadith, the deeds and sayings of the Prophet Muhammad.

21. Sunnis: in Arabic, the word Sunni means "lawful," and its root can be found in Sunna, "the traditional teachings of Muhammad," or "way, course, or teachings." Definitions of Sunni—a member of the branch of Islam that accepts the first four caliphs as rightful successors to Muhammad.

22. Shiite: a Muslim who follows specific religious traditions. Shiites are the second-largest branch of Islam after Sunnis. A Shiite believes that Mohammed's son-in-law, Ali, was his legitimate successor as political and religious leader.

23. Symbolically: in a way that represents something else, purely in terms of what is being represented or implied and as or by means of a symbol or symbolism.

24. Tanakh: the Jewish Scriptures comprising the books of law, the prophets, and collected writings.

25. Theism: belief in the existence of a divine reality, usually referring to monotheism (one God), as opposed to pantheism (all is God), polytheism (many gods), and atheism (without God).

26. Torah: Torah (הרות) in Hebrew can mean teaching, direction, guidance, and law. The most prominent meaning for Jews is that the Torah constitutes the first five books of the Hebrew Bible, namely the books of Genesis, Exodus, Leviticus, Numbers, and Deuteronomy; (also called the *Pentateuch*, "five books" in Greek), traditionally thought to have been composed by Moses.

REFERENCES

1. "Atheist." Merriam-Webster. Accessed February 17, 2022. https://www.merriam-webster.com/dictionary/atheist

2. "Babel." Merriam-Webster. Accessed February 17, 2022. https://www.merriam-webster.com/dictionary/Babel

3. "Bible." New King James Version (NKJV) - Version Information - BibleGateway.com. Accessed October 28, 2024 https://www.biblegateway.com/versions/New-King-James-Version-NKJV-Bible/

4. "Bodhisattva." Encyclopedia Britannica. Accessed February 17, 2022 https://www.britannica.com/topic/bodhisattva

5. "Burqa." Wikipedia. Accessed February 17, 2022 https://en.wikipedia.org/wiki/Burqa

6. "Caliph." Encyclopedia Britannica. Accessed February 17, 2022 https://www.britannica.com/topic/caliph

7. "Caliphate." Cambridge Dictionary. Accessed February 17, 2022. https://dictionary.cambridge.org/us/dictionary/english/caliphate

8. Cusido, Carmen. "4 Types of Intimacy and How to Cultivate Them." Psych Central. Accessed February 17, 2022. https://psychcentral.com/relationships/nourishing-the-different-types-of-intimacy-in-your-relationship

9. "Desire." Dictionary.com. Accessed February 17, 2022 https://www.dictionary.com/browse/desire

10. "Eschatology." Wikipedia. Accessed February 17, 2022
    https://en.wikipedia.org/wiki/Eschatology

11. ""Figuratively vs. Literally." Dictionary.com. Accessed February 17, 2022
    https://www.dictionary.com/e/figuratively-literally/

12. "Hijab." Wikipedia. Accessed February 17, 2022
    https://en.wikipedia.org/wiki/Hijab

13. "Karma." Merriam-Webster. Accessed February 17. 2022.
    https://www.merriam-webster.com/dictionary/karma

14. "Literally." Vocabulary.com. Accessed February 17, 2022.
    https://www.vocabulary.com/dictionary/literally

15. "Mark 16:14-20. Sermon 73. Christ Sends His Workers into His Field." Covenant Orthodox Presbyterian Church. Accessed June 6, 2023.
    https://covenantpensacola.org/2020/07/31/mark-1614-20-sermon-73-christ-sends-his-workers-into-his-field/

16. "Metaphorically." Dictionary.com. Accessed February 17, 2022.
    https://www.dictionary.com/browse/metaphorically

17. "Monk." Vocabuuulary.com. Accessed February 17, 2022
    https://www.vocabulary.com › dictionary › monk

18. "Niq." Wikipedia. Accessed February 17, 2022
    https://en.wikipedia.org/wiki/Niq

19. "Prophetic." Merriam-Webster. Accessed February 17, 2022.
    https://www.merriam-webster.com/dictionary/prophetic

20. "Shite." Vocabulary.com. Accessed February 17, 2022.
    https://www.vocabulary.com › dictionary › Shiite

21. Skeba, David. The Armor of God: Winning the Invisible War. Destiny Image, 2006.

22. "Sunni." Vocabulary.com. Accessed February 17, 2022.
    https://www.vocabulary.com › dictionary › Sunni

23. "Symbolically." Cambridge Dictionary. Accessed February 17, 2022.
    https://dictionary.cambridge.org/dictionary/english/symbolically

24. "Tanakh." Merriam-Webster. Accessed February 17, 2022.
    https://www.merriam-webster.com › dictionary › Tanakh

25. "Theism." PBS. Accessed February 17, 2022.
https://www.pbs.org/faithandreason/theogloss/theism-body.html

26. "Torah." British Library. Accessed February 17, 2022
https://www.bl.uk/sacred-texts/articles/the-torah

27. "What is Philosophy?" What is Philosophy? Accessed February 17, 2022.
https://philosophy.fsu.edu/undergraduate-study/why-philosophy/What-is-Philosophy

28. "What is Sharia law? What does it mean for women in Afghanistan? BBC News. Accessed February 17, 2022.
https://www.bbc.com/news/world-27307249

29. "What Ramadan means, and how to support our Muslim community." Henry Ford College – Future Driven. Accessed February 17, 2022.
https://www.hfcc.edu/news/2021/what-ramadan-means-and-how-support-our-muslim-community

30. White, Mary Gormandy. "5 Main World Religions and Their Basic Beliefs." Your Dictionary. Assessed February 17, 2022.
https://examples.yourdictionary.com/5-main-world-religions-and-their-basic-beliefs.html

ABOUT THE AUTHOR

Apostle Dr. Violet Wallace was born in Jamaica, the sixth child of seven, and was sent to live with her aunt at an early age. During that stay, Apostle realized she had a gift she did not quite understand. As she grew older, she understood that there was a spiritual call on her life. In 1990, she migrated to the U.S. and attended the Bronxwood International Church of God in Bronx, New York, under the spiritual guidance of Pastor Dr. A.G. Quarrie, whose spiritual wisdom helped to shape her life. She had such a passion for souls that she started evangelizing on the train while going to and from work. After seeing herself in a casket for three consecutive weeks, she went to church one Sunday night, and while standing at the pulpit waiting for prayer, she literally died. The ministry leaders prayed for her, she revived, and went home. Through her near death experience, she discovered firsthand God's resurrecting power.

After Apostle's deliverance, the group Intercessor for Christ was born, and she opened her home on Monday nights to strangers, praying for their deliverance, and also went to the homes of those who requested prayer and deliverance. In 1999, Apostle was called by God to start her ministry, and in 2001, Faith in Action Deliverance Ministries was officially incorporated. Her first service was held in her basement with seven attendees. As the ministry grew, the church moved to 237th Street in the Bronx, soon surpassing her expectations. In 2004, she opened Faith in Action Deliverance International Ministries in Spanish Town, Jamaica. And subsequently 62 established Redemption Faith in Action Deliverance Ministries in Sierre Leone, West Africa and Faith in Action Deliverance India, India. Her ongoing work is demonstrated in the Holy Spirit, teaching the undiluted word of God as she operates in the five-fold ministry.

Apostle Wallace is a no-nonsense, down to earth, loving, and compassionate person who will go to the ends of the earth to minister the word of Jesus Christ to a dying world. She has a fervent desire to lead God's people, and she is an energetic preacher who has inspired, informed, instructed, enthused, convicted, and changed the hearts of many people to give their lives to Jesus Christ. Being a motivator, advisor, coach, mentor, teacher, pastor, visionary, and so much more, Apostle Wallace has truly made a lasting impression on the community and the generations to come. Like Paul, she encourages all to be steadfast, immovable, always excelling in the work of the Lord, because their labor is not in vain.

Faith in Action Deliverance Ministries was built on foundational prayers and Intercessory for Christ. Today, it has over 300 members and a multitude of churches. Apostle Wallace once said, "I love to pray for the church and individuals, and for this cause, God poured his spirit in and upon me", thus causing her to become the mouthpiece of God, with an anointing to set the captives free.

www.ingramcontent.com/pod-product-compliance
Lightning Source LLC
LaVergne TN
LVHW052049070526
838201LV00086B/5141